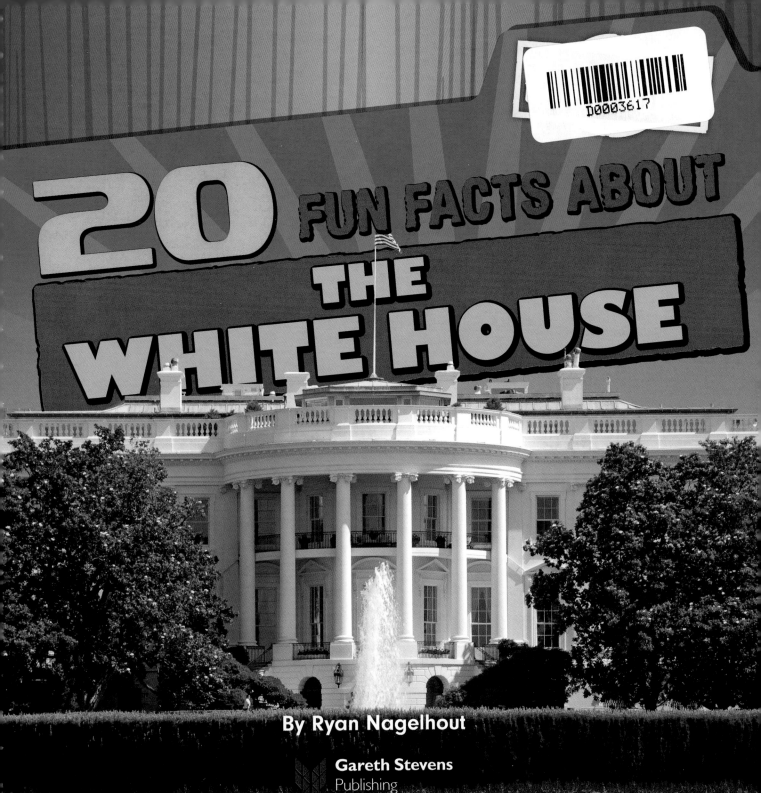

20 FUN FACTS ABOUT THE WHITE HOUSE

By Ryan Nagelhout

Gareth Stevens
Publishing

Please visit our website, www.garethstevens.com. For a free color catalog of all our high-quality books, call toll free 1-800-542-2595 or fax 1-877-542-2596.

Library of Congress Cataloging-in-Publication Data

Nagelhout, Ryan.
20 fun facts about the White House / by Ryan Nagelhout.
   p. cm. — (Fun fact files: US history)
Includes index.
ISBN 978-1-4339-9204-9 (pbk.)
ISBN 978-1-4339-9205-6 (6-pack)
ISBN 978-1-4339-9203-2 (library binding)
1. White House (Washington, D.C.)—Juvenile literature. 2. White House (Washington, D.C.)—History—Juvenile literature. 3. Washington (D.C.)—Buildings, structures, etc.—Juvenile literature. 4. Presidents—United States—Juvenile literature. I. Nagelhout, Ryan II. Title.
F204.W5 N34 2014
975.3—dc23

First Edition

Published in 2014 by
Gareth Stevens Publishing
111 East 14th Street, Suite 349
New York, NY 10003

Copyright © 2014 Gareth Stevens Publishing

Designer: Sarah Liddell
Editor: Greg Roza

Photo credits: Cover, p. 1 Vacciav/Shutterstock.com; p. 5 Richard Nowitz/Digital Vision/Getty Images; p. 6 photo courtesy of Wikimedia Commons, Hoban - White House Design.jpg; p. 7 (White House) Allan Baxter/The Image Bank/Getty Images; p. 7 (Roosevelt) Hulton Archive/Stringer/Hulton Archive/Getty Images; p. 8 photo courtesy of Wikimedia Commons, Chateau de Rastignac.JPG; p. 9 photo courtesy of Wikimedia Commons, PhiladelphiaPresidentsHouse.jpg; p. 10 (left) Dmitri Kessel/Contributor/TIME & LIFE Images/Getty Images; pp. 10 (right), 23 Barry Winiker/Photolibrary/Getty Images; p. 11 Popperfoto/Contributor/Popperfoto/Getty Images; p. 12 MANDEL NGAN/Staff/AFP/Getty Images; p. 13 Chip Somodevilla/Staff/Getty Images News/Getty Images; p. 14 photo courtesy of Wikimedia Commons, L'Enfant plan.jpg; p. 15 photo courtesy of Wikimedia Commons, US $20 Series 2006 Reverse.jpg; p. 16 photo courtesy of Wikimedia Commons, The President's House by George Munger, 1814-1815 - Crop.jpg; p. 17 Greg Mathieson/Mai/Contributor/TIME & LIFE Images/Getty Images; p. 18 Glow Images, Inc/Glow/Getty Images; p. 20 Thomas D. McAvoy/Contributor/Time & Life Pictures/Getty Images; p. 21 Win McNamee/Staff/Getty Images News/Getty Images; p. 22 JEWEL SAMAD/Staff/AFP/Getty Images; p. 24 photo courtesy of Wikimedia Commons, Truman71-305-1.jpg; p. 25 Duncan Walker/E+/Getty Images; p. 26 Brendan Smialowski/Stringer/Getty Images News/Getty Images; p. 27 photo courtesy of Wikimedia Commons, LincolnBedroom05.jpg; p. 29 BRENDAN SMIALOWSKI/Staff/AFP/Getty Images.

Printed in the United States of America

CPSIA compliance information: Batch #CS13GS: For further information contact Gareth Stevens, New York, New York at 1-800-542-2595.

Contents

Words in the glossary appear in **bold** type the first time they are used in the text.

America's House

Near the shores of the Potomac River in Washington, DC, sits the White House, the most famous home in America. Since 1800, the president of the United States has called this building home. For over 2 centuries, presidents have lived and worked in the ever-changing building. They've added rooms and a **balcony**, changed rooms and offices, and even watched the building burn to the ground!

The White House has been home to dozens of presidents, which means there's plenty of history—and mystery—to be found within its sandstone walls.

When leaders from other countries visit the White House, the president often greets them at the south entrance, shown here.

FACT 1

George Washington never lived in the White House.

In 1792, Washington picked **architect** James Hoban's plan for the presidential **mansion**, but he thought it was too small! After a few changes, construction began. It took 8 years to build the White House. Washington died in 1799, 1 year before second president John Adams moved in.

This is Hoban's design for the White House.

Theodore Roosevelt

FACT 2

Teddy Roosevelt made the term "White House" official.

The president's home has been known by many names. It's been called the President's Palace, the President's House, and the Executive Mansion. In 1901, Theodore Roosevelt made "White House" the formal name when he used it on presidential stationery.

Other White Homes

The White House has twins!

Hoban based his White House design on the Leinster House in Ireland. Another twin is a home in France called Château de Rastignac. It likely inspired Thomas Jefferson's additions to the White House in the early 1800s.

Château de Rastignac

The design of the White House itself has been copied many times since it was built.

FACT 4

The White House had a rival.

During the 1790s, Philadelphia, Pennsylvania, was a **temporary** capital city while Washington, DC, was being built. The people of Philadelphia wanted their city to stay the national capital! They built a "President's Mansion" to impress George Washington. However, Washington never lived there.

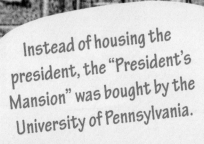

Instead of housing the president, the "President's Mansion" was bought by the University of Pennsylvania.

9

Furniture and Wallpaper

Each president gets to redecorate the White House.

Each new president picks what to put in each room with the help of the official White House **curator**. A secret warehouse in Riverdale, Maryland, houses furniture and artwork that once adorned the many rooms of the White House.

Blue Room, 1940

Blue Room, 2010

FACT 6

The White House once held a yard sale!

In 1882, President Chester A. Arthur **auctioned** off 24 wagonloads of furniture and other White House items to pay for a fancy redecorating. People got very mad! In 1961, Congress made it illegal to remove and sell White House items.

Chester A. Arthur

President Arthur called the White House "a badly kept barracks" before he had it redecorated.

The White Hotel

FACT 7

The rent is free, but the food is not!

The presidential family must pay for its own food, drinks, and laundry service in the White House! State dinners are paid for by the government, but anything else made by the five White House chefs goes on a bill the president pays at the end of the month.

East Room during a fancy dinner

Barack Obama

Barack Obama renovated, or updated, the White House basketball courts in 2009.

FACT 8

The White House is an athlete's dream home.

Sports fans and athletes would love to live in the White House. It has a tennis court, jogging track, swimming pool, billiard room, putting green, and even a bowling lane! Presidents can also play horseshoes.

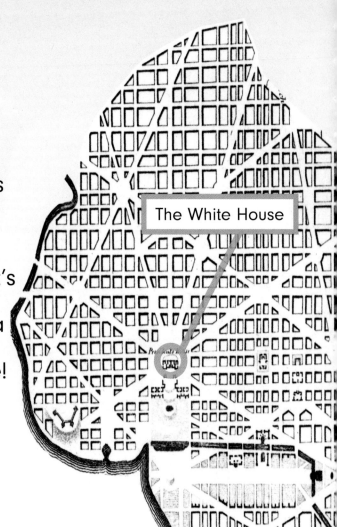

Famous House

FACT 9

The White House is the center of attention in Washington, DC.

When city planner Pierre Charles L'Enfant designed the street plan for Washington, DC, he put the president's house at the center of the city. Over a dozen roads lead to the White House! The largest road runs from the White House to the US Capitol Building.

The White House

The White House appears on money.

In 1929, the White House was added to the back of the $20 bill. A picture of the building's south side was even updated in 1948 to show changes and growing trees! In 1998, the picture was changed to show the north side.

Both sides of the White House have been featured on the $20 bill.

FACT 11

The British burned down the White House in 1814.

During the War of 1812, British troops marched to Washington, DC, and set it on fire. President James Madison fled the White House along with his wife, Dolley. She managed to save a painting of George Washington before she left. It's one of the few things left from the original White House.

This painting shows what the White House looked like after the 1814 fire.

The White House caught fire again in 1929!

On Christmas Eve 1929, President Herbert Hoover had a party at the White House. During the party, a blocked fireplace **flue** started a fire. The West Wing was all but destroyed by the fire, and Hoover himself directed firefighters while important papers were rushed out of the White House.

The 28 fireplaces in the White House have caused some trouble over the years.

Inside the White House

Did you know the White House has four floors? There are many interesting rooms and spaces throughout the White House, including several dining rooms, a flower shop, and a game room where the president can play pool!

CARPENTERS SHOP

BOWLING

FLOWER SHOP

BASEMENT HALL

KITCHEN

SECRET SERVICE

CURATOR

LIBRARY

CENTER HALL

PALM ROOM

MAP ROOM

DIPLOMATIC RECEPTION ROOM

CHINA ROOM

VERMEIL ROOM

VISITORS FOYER

GROUND FLOOR

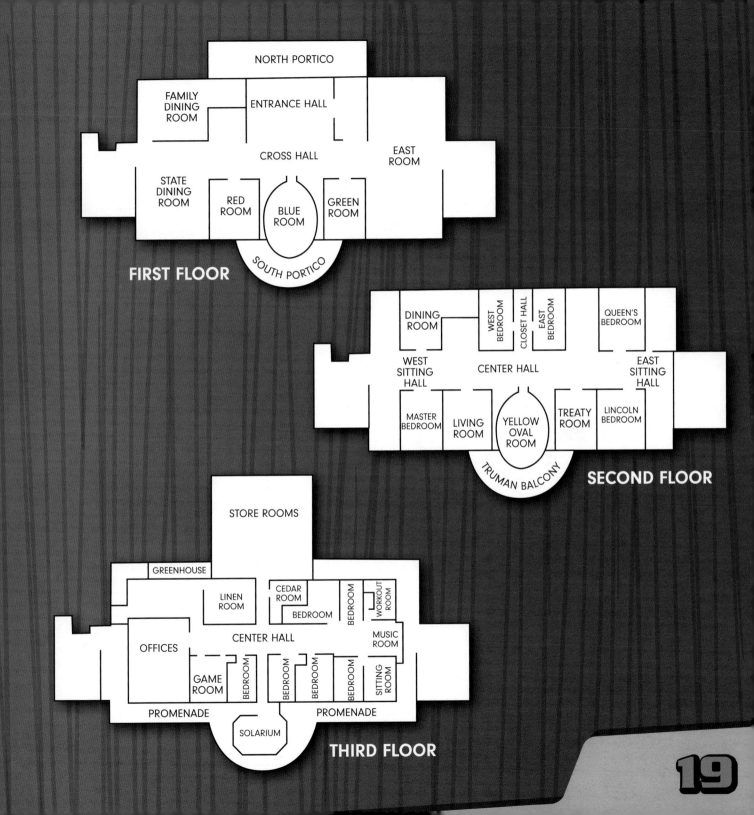

FIRST FLOOR

NORTH PORTICO

FAMILY DINING ROOM

ENTRANCE HALL

CROSS HALL

EAST ROOM

STATE DINING ROOM

RED ROOM

BLUE ROOM

GREEN ROOM

SOUTH PORTICO

SECOND FLOOR

DINING ROOM

WEST BEDROOM

CLOSET HALL

EAST BEDROOM

QUEEN'S BEDROOM

WEST SITTING HALL

CENTER HALL

EAST SITTING HALL

MASTER BEDROOM

LIVING ROOM

YELLOW OVAL ROOM

TREATY ROOM

LINCOLN BEDROOM

TRUMAN BALCONY

THIRD FLOOR

STORE ROOMS

GREENHOUSE

LINEN ROOM

CEDAR ROOM

BEDROOM

BEDROOM

WORKOUT ROOM

OFFICES

CENTER HALL

MUSIC ROOM

GAME ROOM

BEDROOM

BEDROOM

BEDROOM

BEDROOM

SITTING ROOM

PROMENADE

PROMENADE

SOLARIUM

19

It takes 570 gallons (2,160 l) of paint to keep the White House white!

FACT 13

The White House wasn't always white.

The White House walls were built from gray sandstone from a **quarry** in Aquia, Virginia. When the building burned in 1814, only the stone walls were left standing. When it was rebuilt, they painted the stone white to hide any damage from the fire.

Big Changes

The first White House was boring.

James Hoban's plan for the White House was very simple. The porticoes, or porches, that are so familiar today were added much later. James Monroe built the rounded South Portico in 1824, while Andrew Jackson added the squared North Portico in 1829.

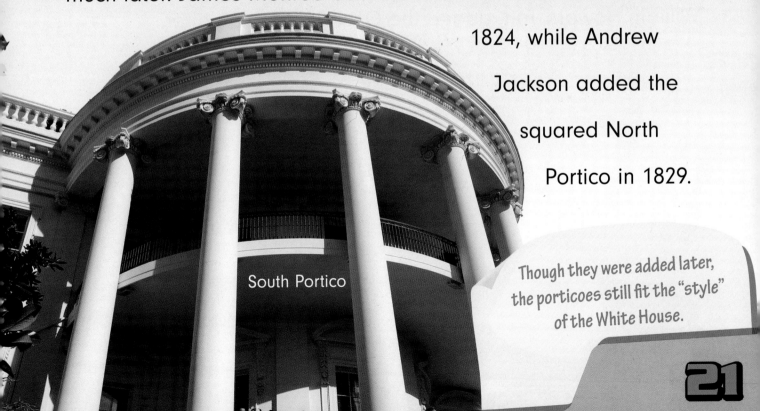

South Portico

Though they were added later, the porticoes still fit the "style" of the White House.

FACT 15

Theodore Roosevelt added the West Wing.

The White House was completely redone while Theodore Roosevelt was in office at the turn of the 20th century. The president's office was moved to the brand new Executive Office Building, now called the West Wing. Roosevelt's successor, William Howard Taft, added the Oval Office soon after.

The Oval Office is the official office of the president.

Blair House hosted many White House guests before Truman stayed there during reconstruction of the White House.

The White House almost fell down.

The White House was almost **condemned** in 1948. The building was so weak most people thought it would fall down, but President Harry Truman ordered major renovations to save it. He added a balcony to the South Portico and lived in nearby Blair House until 1952 when repairs were completed.

FACT 17

The cornerstone of the White House is missing.

After placing the **cornerstone** in 1792, the stone workers celebrated the start of construction with a big party. The next morning, none of them could remember where they put the first stone! People have searched for years but have yet to find the stone and its fancy brass plate.

A steel framework was added to the White House during Harry Truman's presidency.

Some say the White House is haunted.

Presidents, first ladies, and other White House workers have heard and seen some unusual things in the White House. Over the years, people have claimed to have seen the ghosts of former presidents Abraham Lincoln and Andrew Jackson. Some have seen former first lady Abigail Adams carrying laundry!

Abraham Lincoln

Many have claimed to have seen Lincoln's ghost, including British prime minister Winston Churchill.

Rooms to Spare

FACT 19

The White House's rooms are full of color.

The White House has 132 rooms, and many of them are named after colors. Among the most famous are the Green, Red, and **Vermeil** rooms, and the oval-shaped Blue Room. Most of the furniture in these rooms matches their colorful names.

The Red Room is one of the boldest in the entire White House.

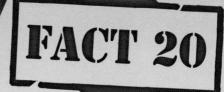

FACT 20

Lincoln never slept in the Lincoln Bedroom.

When Abraham Lincoln was president, the area served as his office. During President Truman's major White House renovation from 1948 to 1952, the area was remade into a guest bedroom named in Lincoln's honor. It's the only room in the White House named after a president.

The Lincoln Bedroom was renovated as recently as 2004.

The Unfinished House

After two fires, major renovations, and secret projects, the White House remains one of the most famous homes in America. It is, however, an ever-changing home. George Washington never called it home, but dozens of future presidents are sure to live at 1600 Pennsylvania Avenue.

American historian William Seale once wrote that "The White House is never finished." And it's true! With each new president come new chairs, tables, and even entire rooms. Much like America itself, the "People's House" is constantly changing.

The White House is constantly changing. What will be added to the "People's House" next?

Glossary

architect: someone who designs buildings

auction: a sale of goods or property at which buyers bid against one another for items

balcony: a platform that hangs off the side of a building and has a railing around it

condemned: declared unfit for use

cornerstone: the first stone of a new building

curator: a person in charge of a collection of things

flue: the part of a chimney where smoke and fire leave the house

mansion: a big, fancy house

quarry: a place where rocks are mined from the ground

temporary: not permanent, lasting for a limited time

vermeil: a reddish-orange color

For More Information

Books

Karapetkova, Holly. *The White House*. Vero Beach, FL: Rourke Publishing, 2009.

National Children's Book and Literacy Alliance. *Our White House: Looking in, Looking Out*. Cambridge, MA: Candlewick Press, 2008.

Silate, Jennifer. *The White House*. New York, NY: PowerKids Press, 2006.

Websites

Inside the White House
www.whitehouse.gov/about/inside-white-house
Learn more about the White House on its official website.

The White House Museum
www.whitehousemuseum.org/
Take a fascinating virtual tour of the White House.

Index